microchips
for
millions

MICROCHIPS

FOR

MILLIONS

JANICE LOBO SAPIGAO

Philippine American Writers and Artists, Inc.
San Francisco, CA

PAWA

ISBN: 978-0-9981792-1-6
LCCN: 2016957188

First printing: 2016
Second printing: 2017
Third printing: 2018
Fourth printing: 2020
Fifth printing: 2021

Cover artwork: Jessica Sabogal
Book design: Edwin Lozada

Published by
Philippine American Writers and Artists, Inc.
P.O. Box 31928
San Francisco, CA 94131-0928
pawa@pawainc.com

www.pawainc.com

Printed in the United States of America.

This project complicates and juxtaposes the "clean" image
of California's Silicon Valley.

The northern part of Santa Clara County and east of
the San Francisco Peninsula are often referred to as the Silicon Valley,
home to many of the world's high technology companies.
The boundaries of the Silicon Valley are not fixed; it is more a regional
state of mind than a geographical location. As an ideal place
of innovation and technological advancement, the Silicon Valley is not
known for its exploitative nature of immigrant women workers
who build it all – those like my mom.

Through the use of binary code, my family's language, Ilokano;
and personal observation, *microchips for millions* draws out the social
layers of the microchip, which are central to the global economy.
I color the moments and questions when a clear glitch in the collusion
of personal, public, private and industrial matters presents itself.
The industry in which she works allows her to create a livelihood
that does not empower her or women like her to ask the questions
that I raise in this text.

This is for my mom.

for the one who taught me the importance of pawis

INTRODUCTION

Risk-taking of the highest order is my personal definition of poetry: formally, linguistically and in all the many ways that poetry demands we take risk. It was this element of risk in Janice Sapigao's poetry that first caught my attention. *microchips for millions*, her first book of poetry, is fraught with risk in a startling and fresh way. It is a work that bravely engages with the very difficult, and often hidden, subject matter of work. "(E)very work day/is a risk/is a truth…," Sapigao writes, and the truth is that workers pay a high and often fatal price so that we can enjoy the fruits of that work in our highly industrialized world. In *microchips for millions*, the workplace is the Silicon Valley, the workers, the highly racialized, female workforce with roots in the Philippines, whose job it is to produce the technology needed for the highly computerized and digitized world we live in.

Sapigao's engagement is forthright and implacable, using her poetry as both searchlight and spotlight, at times seeking out those places we would rather not see: "if the silicon valley is the fold of my mother's palm…," at others focusing her and our attention on this too-often hidden work of immigrant Filipino women like her mother who make the toys of a world gone crazy with technology.

All language is code and Sapigao engages formally with this idea through playing with the different codes she and her poetry negotiate —the foundational binary code of the microchip, the code of her mother tongue Ilokano, the coded language of the factory rules that are designed to protect the chip but which are presented as protecting the workers. The poetry works to reveal the complicated knotted integuments of the global economy, showing us how indeed the personal is the political, is the global, is the industrial, is, indeed, the poem of (in)possibility.

Visually, Sapigao often juxtaposes her text with the relentlessly repetitious appearance of the binary codes, seducing, even contaminating, the reader with their hard-edged macabre beauty.

"(M)y mother is contaminated… her job hurts her…." Mothers are not supposed to be contaminated, in the ordinary course of life, that is, but the extraordinary has now become the ordinary and mothers are contaminated, as are we, the consumers, willing or not, who are contaminated by microchips for millions. It is this leitmotif, this lament for her mother that weaves its way through this work, which experiments at the outer edges of hurt and pain for her mother and all mothers and children caught up in this experiment of life gone awry. It is this lament that grounds the poem and embodies the experience of the experiment of contaminated work.

"(E)very work day/is a risk/is a truth": *microchips for millions* demonstrates the risk that is so often our familiar as poets. And our truth.

M. NourbeSe Philip
Toronto, Canada

00110010 00110000 Questions for Microchips for Millions

an homage

Whose hands do we hold when we hold our devices in our hands?

Whose fingertip zaps into connection with our own as we tap out a quick text?

How do we read the code we cannot read but must read in order to understand what is humanly impossible to understand humanly?

In the non-binary code made in the channel between the indigenous and the immigrant what is expressed inside the language-that-is-be-yond-languageness?

Why are you killing us this way?

Who are the ones—who are the zeros?

Who is an operator, a hand, a unit, a numeral, a deduction, a person?

What is assembled on the assembly line—what does the production line produce?

What plumes, what vapors, what clouds, what suits, what guards, what operates, what dusts, what maps, what swells, what reacts, what absorbs, what consumes, what erases?

Who are the thieves here? Who is the savage of what jungle?

What language is expressed—bacterial, imprinted, circulatory—in the unseen molecular shards we leave behind when we shed our uniforms?

Is the work an effort, an encryption, an endeavor, an enterprise, an experiment, an assembly?

And if code is not binary, but multiple?

Why didn't we know sooner?

Under what circumstances is an object more important than a person?

Who do we see—what do we see—do we see when we see?

Where does stasis or static live in statistic?

Why are you killing us this way?

What knowledge is held in our hands?

What 011010000110000101101110011001000110011 are held in our 011010000110000101101110011001000110011?

Jen Hofer
Los Angeles, CA

Table of Contents

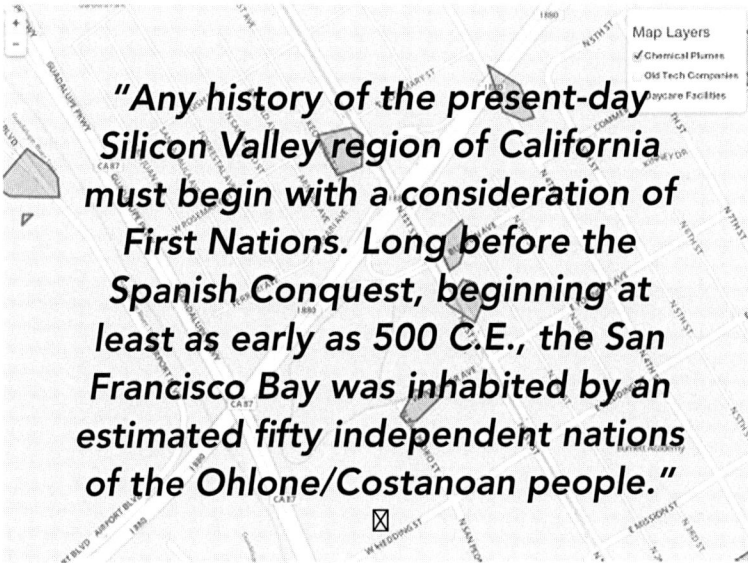

"Any history of the present-day Silicon Valley region of California must begin with a consideration of First Nations. Long before the Spanish Conquest, beginning at least as early as 500 C.E., the San Francisco Bay was inhabited by an estimated fifty independent nations of the Ohlone/Costanoan people."

Let the poetry of this page serve as a moment of recognition
for the native peoples, the Muwekma Ohlone Tribe,
whose lands we inhabit.

0101010001101000011001010010000001000010111000001110000111001001
1011110111000001110010011010010110000101110100011010010110111101101
1110001000000110111101100110001000000100111001100001011101000011010
0101110110011001010010000001001100011000010110111001100100

0100110101100001011011100111100100100000010000110110000101101100010101
1010010101100110011011110111100100110110010101100001011011100010000101
1000011011000110000101011011100110010000110111101101101110110111001100101
1010111001001110011001000000011001000110100010110010000010000001101110
0110110111101110100000100000011101111011000001011011100111101000010000001
0010010110111001100100010110100101100001011011100111001100100000001101
1100011010010111011001101001011011100110011001100000001101110011001
0101110000111010000100000011101000110111100100000011101000110100001
0110010101101101010010110000100000011001101101110010000001110100011
1010000110010101111001001000000110111011011110110101011011000110
0100001000000110110010110111110111010000010000001110011011001010110111
0001101100001000000111001101101101010101101010010101110100011000010110001011001
0110110001100101001000000111000001100001011011001100100110110010101
1011000111001100100000001101111011001000110000010000001101100011000010110
1110011001000010110000011010000101000010110100001010010010010110111
10011001000110100101110110011010010110010110011000111010101100001011011001
01110011001000000111011101101010000110111100100000011101110110010101
11001001100101001000000111011101101010010110110001101110001101001001100
11100110011100100000001110100011011110010000001110011011001010110111100101011011
00011011000010000001110000011000010110110010010010011010010011000110110010101101100
01110011001000000111010001101111010000001110100011010000110010100101001010010010010011011
101000110100001100001010110111000100000001110110110101000011000010111
010000100000011101101100000101110011001100000001100001011011001100011011
0001101111011000110110000101110100011001010010101100100000100000001110001011011000110011011
0001101111011010001101100001011101000110010100010101001000000110000101101100011001100
01110011001000000111010001101111010000110100011010000110010100101001001001001101110
001000000110100011010000110010101100111011011000010000001101100011000010111
100001011011000110010100110111001000000111010001101111010000110100011010000110010100101001001
10000101101110011001100100

Let these pages allow empathy for the immigrant women and their
families whose livelihoods are always, always at stake.

mangirurumen

those who cannot spell hunger
wouldn't dare to experience
those who do and
do without

baba

when the sky falls
and gravity gives in
it becomes grounding

babae

you are wrong
if you think us
below you

the assembly line

011001100110000101100011011
1101000000110100001010

my mother is a fab operator

ma is always on the frontline
of the silicon valley's shadow

01100110011000010110001101
1101000000110100001010

four days a week
ma gets up at four a.m.
boils hot water in a kettle
showers before it screams
ready for coffee
watches the news as she
pulls on her clothes —

jeans and a simple tee
enough to soak up
twelve-hour sweat resting in
orthopedic shoes that
amplify the need for
health benefits & overtime

one of thousands of women
whose nimble fingers and
silenced grumbling spin
microchips for millions
powering laptops and
cell phones that she herself
does not find intuitive enough to use

at the end of every day
she watches the filipino channel
her swollen feet elevated
on the living room couch—
a luxury she buys herself
and her family

"by the early 1980s, filipinos were one of the largest ethnic groups among asian workers at national semiconductor corporation (n.s.c.) in san jose, california." ▨

0110011001100001011000110111 01000000110100001010
ma says she's a fab operator

"this mostly female labor force was appealing to management for a number of reasons: (1) many were fluent in english (2) many had experience working in philippine electronics plants; (3) they had a reputation for hard work; and (4) they were considered obedient to authority." ▨

0011001100110000101100011011110 1000000110100001010
i know she's an assembly line worker

the clean room

in order to come in,
you must first put on:

1.
hairnet

2.
shoe covers

3.
gloves

4.
mask

5.
hood

6.
cover-all

7.
boot covers

8.
goggles

9.
gloves

when you exit,
you must discard:

1.
gloves

2.
goggles

3.
hood

4.
mask

5.
boot covers

*"no, you cannot bring
anything inside the room.
no cell phones,
no watch, no nothing."*

*"you have to go
to the changing room
before you go in to work"*

"i always wear my head band."

*"they don't like you
to wear sneakers.
they like you wear
the shoes they give you.
my feet is hurt"*

*"it's hard to breathe,
sometimes. oh my god"*

*"you can only
call me on
my break, okay?
8:30 or 12:30"*

*"i can only wear t-shirts.
the loose kind for work.
it's better because
you sweat a lot"*

"i can't, balasang. i can't"

*"you have to wear
a suit. goggles.
everything
is covered.
everything."*
*"you can't touch anything.
you have gloves. they will
get mad on you"*
☒

"A clean environment is designed to reduce the contamination of processes and materials. This is accomplished by removing or reducing contamination sources."

⊠

my mother is contaminated

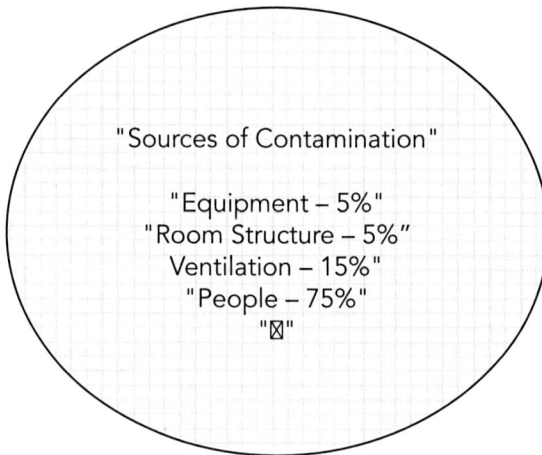

"Sources of Contamination"

"Equipment – 5%"
"Room Structure – 5%"
Ventilation – 15%"
"People – 75%"
"⊠"

"…machines subject silicon wafers to incredibly intense vacuums, caustic chemical baths, high-energy plasmas, intense ultraviolet light, and more, taking the wafers through the hundreds of discrete manufacturing steps required to turn them into CPUs, memory chips and graphics processors." ⊠

"I agree that I will not disclose voluntarily or allow anyone else to disclose either the existence, reason for or contents of this release agreement without the Company's prior written consent, unless required to do so by law. Notwithstanding this provision, I am authorized to disclose this release agreement to my spouse, attorneys and tax advisors on a "need to know" basis, on the condition that they agree to hold the terms of the release agreement in strictest confidence."

X _____   Date: _____
　　　　　　Your Signature

X _____   Date: _____
　　　　　　Printed Name

the family tree

0100110101000101

the social network
planted itself
in my parents' backyard.

01100101011011000110010101100011011101000111001001101111011011100
1101001011000110111001100001101000010100000110100001010

yahoo, google, apple, microsoft, hewlett packard, netapp, fujitsu, sandisk,
adaptec, dust networks, siemens, motorola

0111001001100101011011010110100101101110011001000110010101110010

laptops, pagers, computers, cellular phones, toys, exercise machines

01100101011011100111010001100101011100100111010001100001011010011
01110011011010110010101101110011101 00

electronic arts, netflix, pandora, dreamworks, skywalker sound, lucasfilm,
sony computer entertainment, pandora, zynga

01101001011011100111010001100101011100100110111001100101011101 00

facebook, youtube, linkedin, ask.com, ebay, twitter, lyft, uber

01101001011011100111010001100000101011100100110011001100001011000110110010
1

cupcake, donut, éclair, froyo,
gingerbread, honeycomb, ice cream
sandwich, jelly bean, kitkat

011011110111000001100101011100100110000101110100011010010110111001100110011001000000111001101111001011100110110111010001100101011011010101110011

cheetah, puma, jaguar, panther,
tiger, leopard, snow leopard, lion,
mountain lion, mavericks, yosemite

0110010101101100011001010110001101110100011100100110111101101100
110100101100011011100110000011010000101000001101000010010

sony, logitech, sun microsystems, hitachi, cisco systems, intel, applied materials, philips

011100110110111101100110011010001110111011000010111001001100101

adobe, intuit, symantec, oracle, mcafee, mozilla, palantir technologies, autodesk, dropbox, instagram, songza, pandora, fitbit, gopro

0111001001100101011010001100001011010010110110000001101000010010

walmart.com, gymboree.com, gap.com, levis.com, safeway.com, bebe.com

0111001001100101011011010110100101101110011001000110010101110010

animal implants, automobiles, television sets, digital cameras, stereos, software applications, clouds

0100110101000101

the industrial garden
grows wild, its
abundance infinite.

the valley of toxic fright

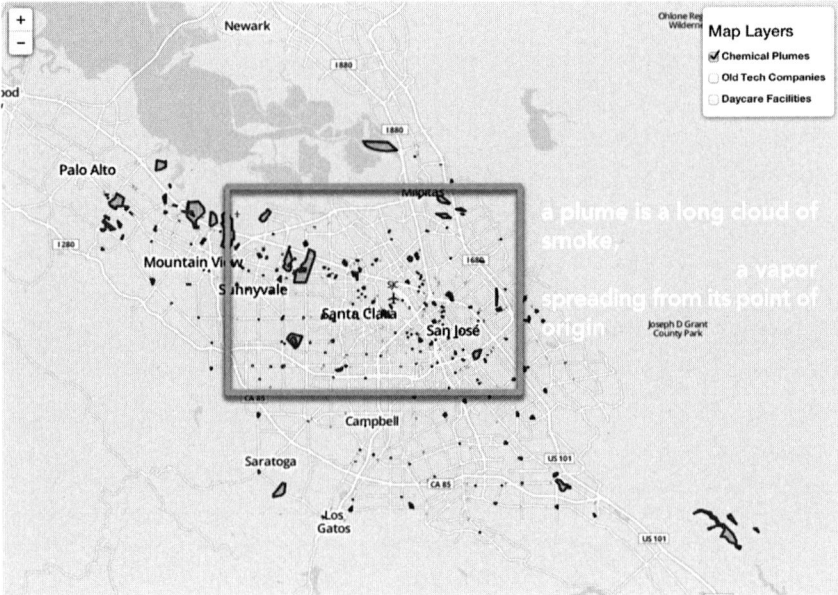

the class

0111001101100011
0110100001101111
0110111101101100
0000110100001010

in college, i took
an environmental racism class
my professor showed a map
of my neighborhood in san jose
with curious red dots next to the
mcdonald's grumma worked at,
near my elementary school, one
north of ma's workplace

0110011001100001011000110111010000001101 00001010

he said the dots
indicated toxic waste sites,
said immigrant women
were on the front line
of exploitation

0111001101100011
0110100001101111
0110111101101100
0000110100001010

half of the professor's
lecture was about
the bunny suit.
he said employees are told
it's to protect them
from chemical harm

011101110110101110111001001101011000011010 0001010

bunny suits
protect the microchips
from human germs

the social network

010010000010011110100110101010001
010000110100001010
ma, auntie glo, uncle cesar, ninang
mely, uncle julius, auntie girlie,
auntie betty, auntie hazel, uncle lito,
uncle camilo, grumma eldang, uncle
islo, auntie fran, uncle boyett

011101110110111101110010011010
110000110100001010
darryl   reports
a   bunny suit,
      hard to breathe in,
funny-looking
                              heavy.

011101110110111101110010011010 11
0000110100001010
my third grade crush
   a neighborhood boy
      darryl street
loved his dirty blonde
mushroom haircut
      he chased me
during   freeze tag

he attended all but one
day of school that year

010010000010011110100110101000
1010000110100001010
darryl's mom, darryl's dad, darryl's
aunt in fremont, darryl's older
brother, darryl's uncle in sunnyvale,
darryl's aunt in sunnyvale

010010000010011110100110101000101
0000110100001010
uncle allos, manang liza, manong
betito, uncle ferdinand, manang
junie, nanang kristine

011101110110111101110010011010
110000110100001010
   wasn't allowed   pictures.
his best friend michael,
   how   cool
         no photos?
next time,   pictures

011101110110111101110010011010 11
0000110100001010
april 25th, 1995
was 'take our daughters
and sons to work day'

010010000010011110100110101000
1010000110100001010
michael's mom, michael's grandpa
on the brink of retirement, michael's
aunt, michael's older cousin

"similar to many of the older, basic manufacturing industries like iron, steel, and auto, entire neighborhoods, friends and families often migrated together into work places." ▨

"…in electronics these familial connections were advantageous to the industry, serving as a form of social control over potential troublemakers." ▨

0111001101100011011010000011 1101101111011011000000011010 000100

0111001101100011011010000011 1101101111011011000000011010 000100

ma used to drop off
my brother and me
at our cousin richard's
until our dad came
to pick us up

auntie pulled me from ma's waist
i didn't want her to leave and
my fingers scraped
the threads of her jeans
of her pants,
clawing air while
ma ran out the door to go to work
and i cried myself to sleep
in a home and blanket
that was not mine

maybe loneliness
maybe her fault

maybe sadness

maybe depression
maybe stress
maybe headaches

"multiple impacts often occur when
entire families and social networks
are employed in the same firm or
industry."
☒

maybe arthritis

maybe gout

maybe bleed i n g g

maybe leukemia

maybe lymphoma maybe it's too late

maybe brain cancer

maybe undiagnosed

maybe loss

maybe death
maybe loneliness

maybe tumors

maybe high blood pressure

maybe their fault

maybe death

because

01000010 01000101 01000011 01000001 01010101 01010011 01000101

if it is the small that runs the company

01000010 01000101 01000011 01000001 01010101 01010011 01000101

if it is the writing that dictates the action

01000010 01000101 01000011 01000001 01010101 01010011 01000101

if microchips are the heart of the revolution

01000010 01000101 01000011 01000001 01010101 01010011 01000101

if women's hands are the movement

01000010 01000101 01000011 01000001 01010101 01010011 01000101

if the silicon valley is the fold of my mother's palms

01000010 01000101 01000011 01000001 01010101 01010011 01000101

if the codes make us complicit

01000010 01000101 01000011 01000001 01010101 01010011 01000101

if technology reflects the speed of human connection

01000010 01000101 01000011 01000001 01010101 01010011 01000101

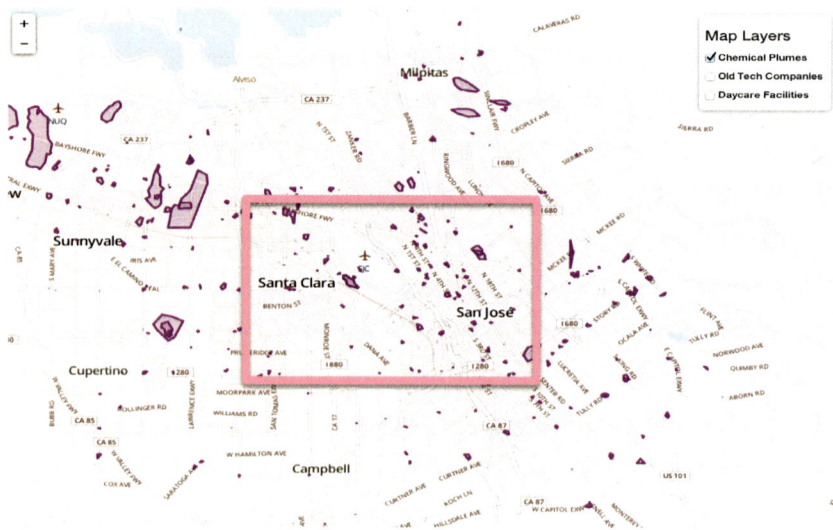

the research

01001101 01000101
how is it that
for as long i've been alive
for as long as my mother has
worked
in the united states,
for as long as i've eaten,
gone to school,
loved her…

01001101 01000101
ma says her co-workers
don't like her because
her lead constantly asks her
to work overtime
and ma always signs up
for the most days to work.

01001101 01000101
"she get mad at me for working
on thursday, friday and saturday.
she said she wanted one of my days,
so i said, go, take my saturday.
she said she wanted my thursday.
i said, no, how come
you don't sign up earlier?"
⊠

01001101 01000101
how is it that i lived for so long
without detecting how
her job hurts her?
why didn't i know sooner?

"i am a good worker.

i

i

i w

i w

i w   o

i wo

r

i wo

rk

i go

i g o

o

i good

i01110011011000110110100001101111011011110110110000 00110100001010 good

i work hard."

☒

the games

have a stadium of seats.

"you come from one of the more storied franchises in the history of
professional football"

– ric "nature boy" flair ⌧

ma's favorite football team
lives closer to her house
yet she has never been
farther from
ever being able
to afford tickets

friends remark
that they can buy food
using an app
from their seats
or cell phones

the stadium is known for
being open and airy, and
environmentally friendly.

the connections

my homegirl lily
created a short film
about her mother,
also a fab operator.

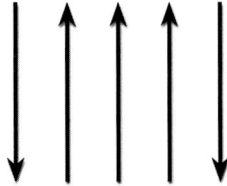

as soon as i saw photos
of her mother smiling
in her bunny suit, i cried.
tears really do swell,
a blanket of water
falling from the bed of my vision
and onto the classroom table.

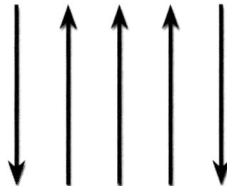

0011001100110000101100011011101000000110100001010

during the q & a session,
lily cried so much
that she could not talk,
the memory crowding,
a fluid rounding and inflating.

the need

01100011 01111001 01100001 01101110 01101001 01100100
01100101 00101100 00100000 01100001 01110010 01110011
01100101 01101110 01101001 01100011 00101100 00100000
01101110 01101001 01110100 01110010 01101001 01100011
00100000 01100001 01100011 01101001 01100100 00101100
00100000 01101000 01111001 01100100 01110010 01101111
01100011 01101000 01101100 01101111 01110010 01101001
01100011 00100000 01100001 01100011 01101001 01100100
00101100 00100000 01111000 01111001 01101100 01100101
01101110 01100101 00101100 00100000 01110011 01101001
01101100 01101001 01100011 01100001 00101100 00100000
01101100 01100101 01100001 01100100

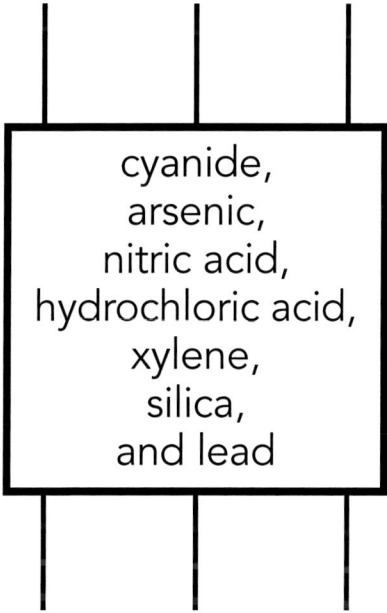

cyanide,
arsenic,
nitric acid,
hydrochloric acid,
xylene,
silica,
and lead

these can be found in your devices. all are centuries-old noted forms of poisons.

⊠

the praise

01110111011010000111001000011010000010101010

my mother builds
the backbone of the silicon valley
you can say she's
single-handedly responsible
for the microchip revolution

my mother   is a step ladder

is a spine
      is a skeleton   is a muscle

is a labor force   is vertebrae   is a staircase
is the key to a multi-millionaire's business
                                is a person.

01110111011010000111001000011010000010101010

all hail
the silicon valley
may you all endlessly
power up,
aggregate the future,
sip the coffee made
by your interns,
and allow me
to ask sincerely,

why

0111011101101000011110010000110100001010

0111011101101000011110010000110100001010

are

0111011101101000011110010000110100001010

you

0111011101101000011110010000110100001010

killing

0111011101101000011110010000110100001010

0111011101101000011110010000110100001010

us

0111011101101000011110010000110100001010

this

0111011101101000011110010000110100001010

way

0111011101101000011110010000110100001010

0111011101101000011110010000110100001010

0111011101101000011110010000110100001010

the source

"Remember, these were just people who needed a job."
⊠

sunlight outlines
dust particles,
angles rainbows
from hair strands

we can count
dirt like stars,
fluttering and floating
in day time.

we drop germs:
oil and grease,
specks and slivers,
cream and polish,

wax and scraps
into the air.
fibers fall from faces,
eyelashes and hands

expensive contact
if not prevented.
workers give guidance,
lessen the fear

they are guardians
against risk,
they keep away
the kind of air

that permits
forgetting to breathe

the justice

auntie coring was fired today.
ma said the supervisors
saw surveillance footage
of her holding the wafer fabs
with 00110110101101001011000110111
001001101111011000110110100001101
001011100000000110100001010

through her gloves

she transferred the wafer
from one machine to the next
in lieu of automation
she gesticulated
a craning claw
with her right hand –
the injustice recorded
from a corner camera,
replayed for all
co-workers to fear

if cameras are singular in scope,
what might we say about those
who use them to source full truth?

you're supposed to wait for
you should watch the machine
you should never touch
the 00110110101101001011000110111
001001101111011000110110100001101

001011100000000110100001010

"we saw it. they caught her."

*but how come no one saw
auntie coring's indictment
as unfair; how she became
        criminal*

*"she got no warning. just fired.
like that."*

just

        like

                                011101000110
                                100001100001
                                011101000000
                                110100001010

and i wonder if ma is scared

*"she's the second one.
they fired someone else
two months ago.
a vietnamese [woman]."*

...and this one?

*"she's filipino. my friend.
but oh well. what you gonna do?"*

and i wonder if ma
will make it to retirement

without being fired for nothing

without cancer

without pulling from her 401k

without   011101000110
           100001100001
           011101000000
           110100001010

and i wonder if justice
is living without punishment
or slowly righting the wrongs

*"lithography is the process of
printing from a flat surface treated
so as to repel the ink except
where it is required for printing. in
electronics, it is a method for
making printed circuits."*

0110011001100001011000110111010000001101000001010

my mother is a lithographist

⊠

*"to make the clean room
[exhibit]
more conducive to learning,
attempts should be made to
remove the feeling of
untouchability and sterility."*

my mother is an object

the tech museum of innovation 1993

01101010011011110110101101100101000
0110100001010
i remember
the field trip where ma
was   invisible   artist,
        chaperone
hand-holder   exhibits
        her   work

the color and projects
the classmates and questions
the buttons and walking
the feeling of getting lost
and not being harmed

the tech museum of innovation 2006

the 'in the clean room' exhibit
showcases   videos   signage
            etcher   stepper
        microscope
                    wafer board making
        buttons   plexiglass
i remember it empty no one
        but me and my brother
cousin   , "this is where
    ma works!"
                        plexiglass

how you are hanging on the wall
        how there is no kinship here
    how the boots fall over in a locker
how her livelihood is on display

    how the very process you mimic
how machines work as you watch
        how children cannot see,
                    cannot play with
how you cannot ~~fathom dream~~
~~imagine feel empathize care help~~
                                touch
        how no one wishes
            for this 0110101001101111
01101011011001010000110100001010

the tech museum of innovation of 2012

0110101001101111011010110110010100001101
00001010

the 'reactable' exhibit is
an interactive tabletop
microchips control a blending
of global music in the auditorium

0110101001101111011010110110010100001101
00001010

'reface' combines visitors'
eyes, noses and mouths
by random and deliberate choices
to make various expressions

0110101001101111011010110110010100001101
00001010

      we took a picture of us
          taking a picture of us
           taking a picture.

0110101001101111011010110110010100001101
00001010

'resolution' allows visitors
to play with physical pixels;
children spell their names
each hand-held piece
its own computer

011101110110100001111001

even
       though

  we are   small

    do

        you
       see

       us?

the person

01101011011001010000110100001010

ma's favorite colors
are yellow and blue.
for as long as i've known her,
these haven't changed.

01101011011001010000110100001010

call her ma,
but her real name is felicitacion.
it means congratulations
in french and spanish.

ma says my grumpa casiano
and grumma lourdes named her
felicitacion
because she was
born on new year's day.

01101011011001010000110100001010

she likes shopping
in the clearance sections
of ross and marshall's stores.
she likes filipino game shows
and crushes on
former bay area
weatherman john farley.

her favorite book is "i don't know,
balasang. komiks?"

01101011011001010000110100001010

she was born in 1952
in alo-o, umingan,
pangasinan, philippines.
when i asked her,
"what schools did you attend?"
she said, "are you
interviewing me again?
i have to go to the bathroom."

01101011011001010000110100001010

i can't catch her
but i always have her.

01101011011001010000110100001010

ma has two sisters and
two brothers in the bay area,
and two sisters who passed away
during world war two.

when people die,
ma always says,
"they forgot to breathe."

she came to the
united states in 1978.
she came with her sister
they stayed with her parents
and brother; all of them
were new immigrants
sharing a small house
in san francisco, california.

011010110110010100001101000001010

ma's first job
was for twin industries,
another electronics manufacturer.

her first car was a ford mustang,
a car she misses especially
when she shows me pictures
011010110110010100001101000001010

surat

scratches of thinking
shooting word blanks
undoing the unconscious
with each

wayas

where what's yours
depends on others
recognizing how much of it
you deserve

oras

i'm here but
i'm trying to be
somewhere else
up and away

the start-up

0111010001110110
the bravo network hosts
"the real housewives" series,
"project runway", "milliondollar
listings", "top chef" and
a new show called
"start-ups: silicon valley."

01110011011001010110010
10000110100001010
the first episode
of the season
boasted young entrepreneurs
from palo alto who geeked
at coding, algorithms
and toga parties.

0111010001110110
"silicon valley isn't a town,
a neighborhood, or a zip code
it's a concept; the epicenter
for the most revolutionary
advances in technology
where the future of tomorrow
is being created today."

University Avenue

one of the show's characters,
another character,
sarah, age 25,
lived in palo alto's four
seasons hotel
        just because.
she said that the silicon valley
is all about "not what you
know,
but who you know."

01110011011001010110010
10000110100001010
one of the show's characters,
hermione, age 25, said
business meetings were
not that serious;
t-shirts and flip flops
were requisite work attire

101

011
000
11
011
011
00
011
000
01
011
100
11
011
100
11
001
000
00
011
001
00
011
010
01
011
100
11
011
100
00
011
000
01
011
100
10
011
010
01
011
101
00
011
110
01

the US-101 freeway parallels the four seasons hotel and my former workplace, dividing palo alto and east palo alto by a bridge and an IKEA.

east palo alto is situated
at the base of the
dumbarton bridge.

the tech boom
of the early 1990s
did not happen
to east palo alto.

in 1992, e.p.a. had the worst
murder rate in the united
states due to drug-related
crimes

the first supermarket came
to the city in 2009, ending its
food desert status.

students from here struggle
with school and people not
from here wonder why.

01101101011001010000110
100001010
i worked at college track:
where black, latina/o, and
pacific islander youth did
their homework every day
after schoo l.

the organization's founder
is laureen powell jobs,
widow of steve jobs, the
founder of apple, inc.

the silicon valley
is the unforgivable wealth
on the backs
of the impoverished,
the toxic idea of those
in search of a playground
for a recycled american dream,

in the shadows of start-ups
        a place for my mother

map not drawn to cartographic or traumatic scale

Freeways often divide people and their homes by race, age, skill level, and income.

the union

011101110110100001111001000011010000010
10

my mother's boss
was fired today
after nineteen years
with the company,
they cited failure
to meet deadlines
and production goals

…and ma doesn't know
what they're talking about
because they've worked over time and
they've scheduled
less workers

and ma asks
if i were her
would i fight?

…and ma always fights.

011101110110100001111001000011010000010
10

her boss told them not to
that speaking out was
risking their jobs
that human resources
doesn't like questions

011101110110100001111001000011010000010
10

the silicon valley is largely anti-union
the long hours,
rule-breaking,
hiring practices,
and runaway jobs
would be unjust
under labor laws.
my mother sees patterns,

says the new CEO is from intel,
that he hires anyone
who's worked there.
ma jokes that even her workplace
has intel inside.

ma and her co-workers
come together to raise funds
print flyers and
meet secretly
to throw
                their former boss
                            a pizza party.

the games

"the warriors are giving up something with their move, with the bay area changing, though...there's a good thing going in oakland right now, that's all i know, and it's being given up for something shinier and more lucrative. those aren't synonyms for worse. just different." – grant brisbee

even my precious dubs
are being offered
to sell (out) their home
for an upgrade to the city
and a view of the water

who knew that sports teams
could be gentrified, lured away
from communities who support
losses, trades, and mistakes?

while oracle arena sits in
industrial oakland,
among working-class
folks, fans, and families;
a move to san francisco
raises questions. who will
be televised and in
whose hometown?

no rest / no more

chop hot microchips / hot rooms /

mothers in millions /

mothers' hips /

sim others' chips —.

he tom his ion ions .

slim shot to some so

mill them hem them

mesh mot his me

more millions

millions o moms

mother in

her hot room mother shot some ions others cop hots nil rest
mes mots ship chips ship to them tom he some to them on
others no homes in sin son s e s t o p n o m o r e p l l s n o

"The chemicals were in a language I didn't understand. You'd have to have a much higher education than I had to understand what the words meant," she said. "I couldn't even spell them to look them up in my dictionary." — Alida Hernandez, former IBM clean room worker

"If you protect the product, by default, you protect the people." - *Chris Corpuz, Health and Safety Consultant in the Silicon Valley*

NaCn	As	HNO$_3$	HCl		

ni! hips stop shop / moms is
set in / chop om chop / on to
slim s h i t / s t o p i t / o o o

☒

the scare

today, ma told me that she
had a second mammogram
after not telling me about the first
she said it was scary

that a machine
clinched her breast and
found extra fluid
…and i thought about

all of the articles i'd read:
the testimonies from women
whose livelihoods were lost
to numerous 01100011 01100001
01101110 01100011 01100101
01110010 01110011
and workroom dangers

she said she was scared
and asked me what
would have happened
if they'd found something?

i stared at the pink of her eyes
and thought about how
i'd written too slowly –

that i, too, would lose
my livelihood to a
social 01100011 01100001
01101110 01100011 01100101
01110010 of silencing

…and i was scared to a fault,
convinced that my research
yielded too much data
and not enough results

ma said they found nothing
after this second time
and i remembered
how every work day

        is a risk
       is a truth
    we treat too loosely
what would have happened
if they'd found something?

if they found something and
announced it
before i did.

what if she had 01100011 01100001
01101110 01100011 01100101 01110010?

52

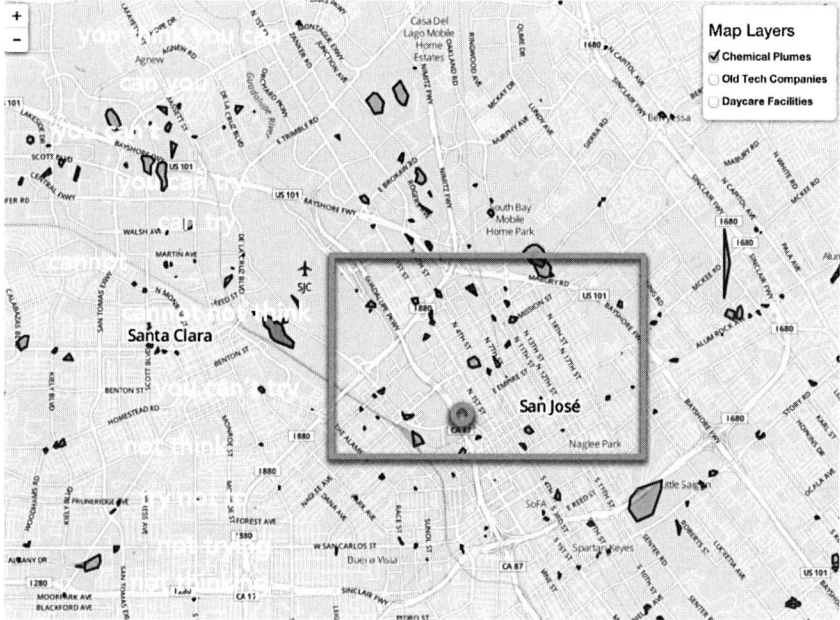

the company picnic

every six months
at christmas time
or summertime
ma's company shells out
hot platters
of breakfast or dinner
on a saturday
employees are limited
to bringing two guests

ma introduces me
to her co-workers
whose names
are nothing like the
passive aggressive nicknames
she'd assign them in our talks

they all greet us
introduce their children
and friends

everyone smiles

as though

it's allowed

a relief from

normalcy

they play games
eat it's it ice cream
hold raffle tickets
take pictures with
hired santa claus or
some cartoon character

'the lady who doesn't like to work'
is elma

'the only guy in our department'
is quy

'the lady the old lady who should
retire'
is vivian

'the tall, white man'
is the new boss

'the indian guy'
is a nice engineer

there's always one table
elevated on a stage
where men sit
all patrons i've never met
the company's managers
play poker with
colored tokens
while their employees
frantically gather
game tickets
for airline tickets,
televisions, dvd players,
ipads, and laptops,
or wine tours.

ma shouts
at me,
"hey!
you go play
so we can win something!"

the woman behind the microchip

ma said
she went on break
while her supervisor
looked for her
before she could
get back in her bunny suit
she was whisked away
into an office
with whom she calls
the big boss

and they cited
products not working,
employee reduction efforts
and needing to let her go

when asked if she had
any questions, ma asked
maybe not knowing her rights,
"can i file for unemployment?"

and my heart broke for her,
a fracture and shard
unanswered questions

she smiles and says
she will be okay
'i will work anywhere'

but i know this market
like i know ageism
and people who pretend
to like immigrants

i know my mother
works hard.

and i know
a company that
does not.

she loses her job
everyday that she is
without one.

the headlines

1. October 16, 2014: *Mercury News:* bay area apartment rents at record high

2. April 17th, 2015: *Curbed New York* renting in manhattan sucks, but the bay area is worse

3. July 15th, 2014: *Mercury News:* bay area apartment rents continue relentless rise on tight supply

4. October 22nd 2014: *Curbed San Francsco:* it's official: bay area rents are absolutely crushing new york's

5. October 23rd, 2013: *KQED:* priced out: the bay area's high cost of living

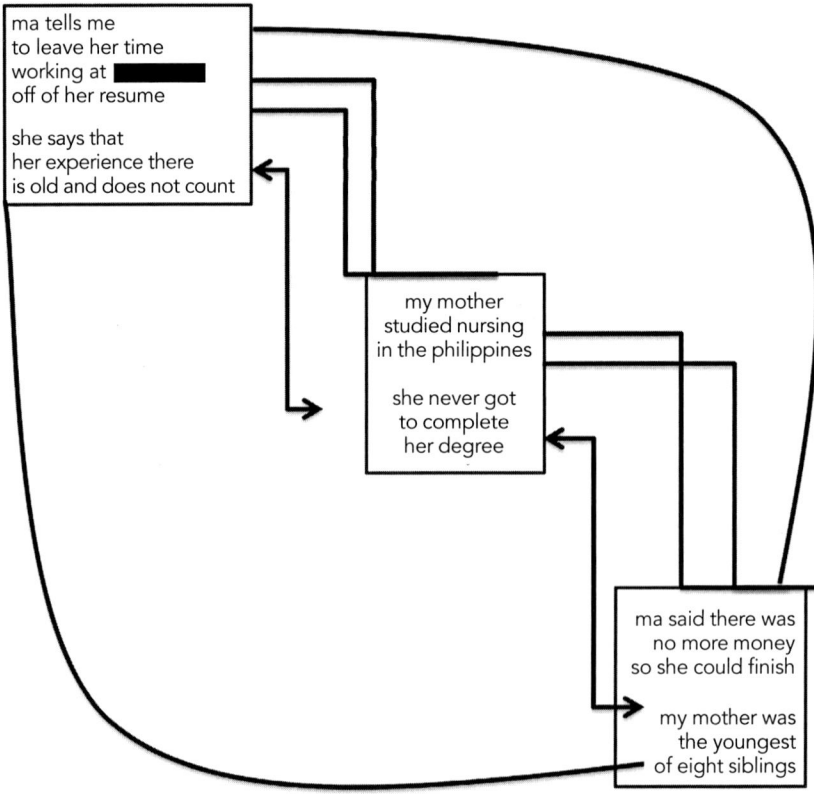

ma tells me
to leave her time
working at ▮▮▮▮▮▮
off of her resume

she says that
her experience there
is old and does not count

my mother
studied nursing
in the philippines

she never got
to complete
her degree

ma said there was
no more money
so she could finish

my mother was
the youngest
of eight siblings

the games

"fans in silicon valley expect more in their sports venues, so we wanted to make sure this stadium had innovation and fan engagement at the highest level" – dave kaval

can you evict the act
of redlining?

these games draw lines
between crowds
i am one of many
who wonder,
how come the silicon valley
squats on san josé?

much of this make-believe
results in real-life dangers

when you are designing,
and urban planning our future,
do you think of people
with allegiance,
with loyalty,
with pride –
without the business
of fandom?

"I may have obtained confidential, proprietary and trade secret information, including information relating to the Company's products, plans, designs and other valuable confidential information. I agree not to use or disclose any such confidential information."

the cry

ma,

tell them we go to church on sundays

tell them spending christmas together

is a tradition we need to start soon

tell them about the blisters behind your ankles

or the calluses that outline your step

tell them about your queendom

that you can't preside over your people if you're not home

tell them buildings are a poor substitute for sunlight

tell them about living paycheck-to-paycheck

tell them about your arthritis

tell them that i ripped your beltloops when i was six

clawing onto you because i didn't want you to go to work that day

tell them about how starting your shift is a sentence and

punching out your timesheet is freedom

tell them you're sick today

that you're sick of them every day

that work is not a place without a place to sit

that free snacks and more hours don't fool you

tell them that microchips don't have feelings

tell them about your garden

and how soil reacts to water

how you chip off thorns with uneven fingernails

or how your orchids finally bloom yellow, pink and purple

tell them they can't automate your spirit

tell them they can't outsource your humanity

tell them dignity is priceless

tell them you miss the mid-day radio

tell them you miss the price is right

tell them that it's confidential

tell them machines performing over 1,000 chemical reactions are dangerous

tell them they're hazardous

tell them what the doctors said

      how your knees creak

            how dad massages your feet every night

tell them we don't care about who they are

      since they do not know us

tell them in ilokano

tell them in tagalog

      or vietnamese

         or spanish

           or khmer

tell all of your co-workers, my aunties

tell them to say no

tell them you say no

tell them no

      you're not going to work today

      you're not going to work

tell them that today

      the silicon valley resigns

         tell them you run the town

tell them that they work for you!

tell them no

      hell   !

tell them   01101110 01100011 01100101 01110010

                         more

    01101110 01101111 00001010

ngata

dazed beginnings
to sound out sense
your tongue falling off the roof

kita

your gaze latches onto
a distant shine
that one! no, that one!
yes, it is looking back

ramay

the smallness between air
color tips of body
line segments of hard work
in action

the past

my cousin richard told me
he writes poetry
that he's finishing a book
i haven't looked at yet

that i forgot   that i haven't bothered

that i've been too busy

i told him i was, too –
that it's about how

our mothers made microchips
when they used to work together   at national?
the bunny suits   you mean hazmat suits?

you mean circuit boards?

the wafer plates   yeah, they were always gone.
the reason why they left us
early in the morning
or right before bedtime

– he told me he didn't know   after twenty years
after all this time playing
on the consoles of our past:

nintendo entertainment system

sega genesis   nintendo entertainment system

playstation

nintendo 64

that our parents had masterminded them before we could
a green game boy

game gear
that they were on the next level
playstation 2
x box
that the gaming industry does not preclude them   x box 360
playstation 3
wii
playstation 4

a nintendo ds

a playstation portable

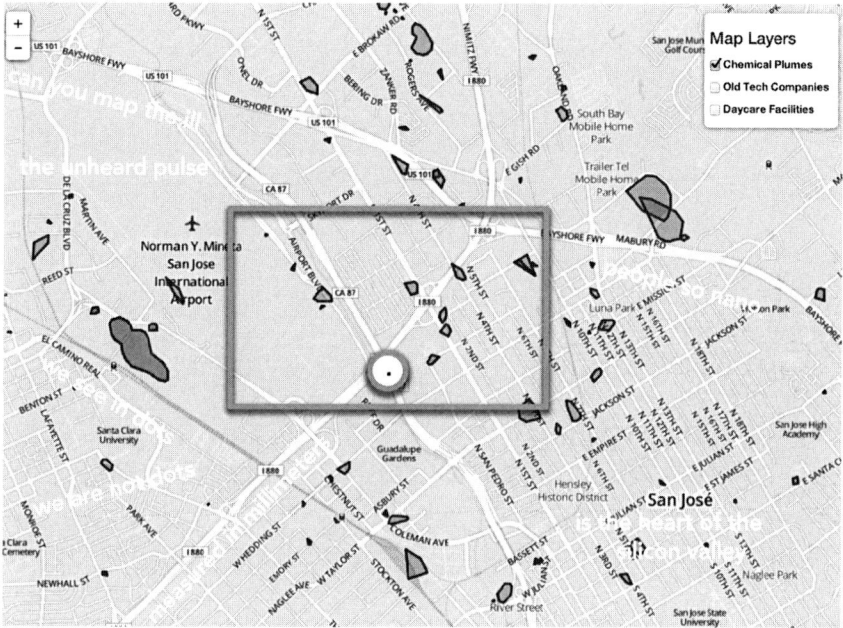

Moore's Law is a prediction made by former Intel founder, Gordon Moore, that states that computer chips will double their speed and power every eighteen to twenty-four months. Moore's Law came true.

the headlines

6. April 4th, 2015: *SF Gate:* felons barred from constructing apple's campus

construction workers who have been charged with a felony or those with pending felony charges are banned from working on building at apple. this is unusual for construction workers.

who are the thieves here? is apple's latest discovery the space inside us where we further punish the punished? is its greatest invention the canyon between its seven hundred and thirty billion dollar value and its homeless citizens?

7. December 14th, 2014: *San Jose De-Bug:* exodus from the jungle: the story of that morning

the jungle was located on story road across from happy hollow park and zoo. it was one of the largest homeless encampments in the united states. there were close to 400 residents at the time of its dismantling. on december third, the city of san josé sent contracted cleaning crews and police to remove the residents and their possessions.

if you have never had to hold
your home in your hands or if
you have never seen your
home bulldozed seconds
after you left it or if the
streets are just a place for
you to drive on then who is
the savage of what jungle?

8. december 13th, 2014: *National Public Radio:* in a divided san francisco,
private tech buses drive tension

"the resentment about — oh, people
have high-paying jobs caused by the
tech industry, and that's displacing,
and rent prices and home prices are
going through the roof, and I guess
the buses are a visible sign of all
that," a tech worker said.

"you can blame me if you want, but I
don't think I'm really the cause of the
problem."

"people feel that if you have worked
hard enough, that's why you are
successful and you have this great
job and you get to live in this great
place."

i cannot american dream
my way out of poverty
just as i cannot white
imagine that there is not
suffering where i live.

the toxic city

> The greater the power and speed of our electronics devices, the greater the need for women workers.
>
> The Silicon Valley cannot exist without the work, power, and presence of immigrant women.

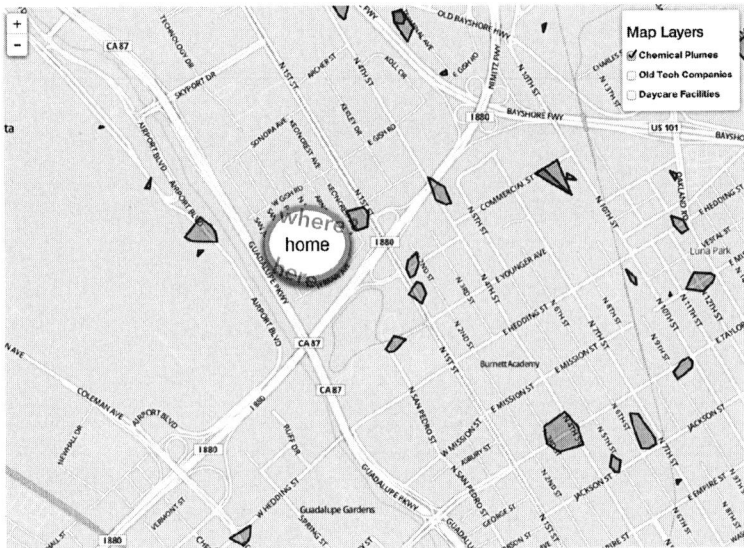

Map Layers
☑ Chemical Plumes
☐ Old Tech Companies
☐ Daycare Facilities

where
home
is

what do we do with
     a map?
                                    don't act
               again
                                slighted

if we stare
                          if my h   me
     at injury

                    long enough
                             it will heal

  right
 t   xic neighborhood   my childh od
     where does it go
             does the sky absorb

             do humans consume
do the plumes move

          do scars erase   again.

do wounds die

Acknowledgements

⟬ Love to Philippine American Writers and Artists, Inc. (PAWA). Many thanks to Edwin Lozada and Barbara Jane Reyes.

⟬ Thank you to my girl, Jessica Sabogal, for the beautiful cover art.

⟬ Thank you to Ngoho Reavey and Mike Wendt of Woodland Pattern in Milwaukee, WI for publishing a chapbook of this work, *toxic city* (tinder tender press, 2015).

⟬ Some of these poems have appeared in *Issue 4* of *macaroni necklace*, *Issue 19, Autumn 2015* of *Action, Yes!*, *KQED Arts*, *TAYO Literary Magazine*, *Cheers From the Wasteland*, the *Silicon Valley De-Bug Poetry Mixtape*, and *END/PAIN*. Thank you to the editors and organizers.

⟬ Much gratitude to the folks who've organized the following reading venues, and have allowed a girl like me to read: (KSW) Kearny Street Workshop's APAture, Sunday Jump, Hazel Reading Series, PAWA x KSW National Poetry Month, Featherboard Writing Series, Split This Rock, the Silicon Valley De-Bug Summer of Discontent program and the Filipina/o American International Book Festival.

⟬ These are important community spaces for writers of color, experimentation, and scholar-activists: Voices of Our Nation (VONA) Conference, Kundiman, Jack Kerouac School of Disembodied Poetics Summer Writing Program at Naropa University (this place is full-circle magic), UCSD Ethnic Studies, Kamalayan Kollective, and the Association of Asian American Studies (where I first read from this work in San Francisco).

⟬ M. NourbeSe Philip, your guidance and light made this book possible.

⟬ For Bel, Shana, UCSD CCC, Kandi, Kwame, Deanna, Tinesha, Jet, Ed, Steph, Eddy, Melissa, Al, CIPHER, the Kababayan Learning Community, Liza, Grace, Kim, Von, Nate, Sol, John, Marlon, Char, Cary, Bella, Denise, April, Caz, Carmela, Paola, Nic, Michelle, Jason, Kazumi, Yael, Kirstie, Liezl, Malou, Marcus, Gladys, Philip, Tep, Trish, Carla, Frida, Janelle, Mike, Erin, Big Red, Maria, Brent, Marleina, Gwen-Florelei, K., Jess, Lianna, Cynthia, Rachelle, Wendy, Matt, and all y'alls parents; the folks of Kabataang maka-Bayan (KmB Pro-People Youth). For #ALTJAMS.

ॐ Vejea Jennings, Jason Magabo Perez, Professor K. Wayne Yang, and Professor Yẹn Le Espiritu were especially instrumental on my path to my M.F.A.

ॐ To the faculty at CalArts and the Writing Program classes of 2011, 2012, and 2013: thank you all for an anomalously beautiful M.F.A. experience.

ॐ To the baristas and friends at Crema Coffee Roasting Co., Swork, Roy's Station Coffee & Tea, Urth Caffe, and Chimney Coffee House.

ॐ To my students who push, challenge, and build community. We have so much work to do.

ॐ To Lorenz, Quynh, Liz, and Fernando.

ॐ To Paolo: I love you for your patience, understanding, and criticality.

ॐ To my family: Willard, my fav. bro; my dad(s) who I think about and miss; Richard, my other brother; all the Lobo fam who baby me, and all of the Sapigao and Sabio fam who've reached out to me.

ॐ Of course, for Ma. #mymommakesthevalley.

⊠ **citations are (mostly) in order of appearance**

pp. 13, 24, 32, 53, 65, 70

"The Chemical Legacy of Old Silicon Valley." *NBC News Bay Area*. Web. 1 Jun 2014.

pp. 13, 15

"Secularization of the Missions, Mexican Land Grants and the Establishment of the East Bay Rancherias During the American Conquest Period." *Muwekma Ohlone Tribe of the San Francisco Bay Area*. Web. 3 Jan 2015.

pp. 18, 27, 28

Park, Lisa Sun-Hee and David Naguib Pellow. *The Silicon Valley of Dreams: Environmental Injustice, Immigrant Workers, and the High-Tech Global Economy*. New York: NYU Press, 2002.

p. 19, 21, 29, 30, 39, 44, 60

Somera, F. Lobo. Personal interview. 2011.

p. 20

Vijayaraghavan., M.N. "Clean room, wet bench. Semiconductor Clean Room Intro" *The Center of Excellence in Nanoelectronics*. Bangalore, India: Indian Institute of Science, 2011.

Snyder, Jon. "A Chip is Born: Inside a State-of-the-Art Clean Room." Wired.com. Web. 3 Jan 2015. http://www.wired.com/2010/10/inside-a-state-of-the-art-cleanroom/

p. 33

WWE. "Nature Boy Ric Flair inspires the San Francisco 49ers." Online video clip. Youtube.com, 5 January 2014. 6 January 2014.

p. 50

Brisbee, Grant. "Where the Warriors fit in the messy, changing Bay Area." *SBNation.com*. Web. 19 May 2015.

ABOUT THE AUTHOR

Janice Lobo Sapigao is a writer, poet, and educator. She is a VONA/Voices Fellow and was awarded a Manuel G. Flores Prize – PAWA Scholarship to the Kundiman Poetry Retreat. She is the Associate Editor of *TAYO Literary Magazine*, and a co-founder of Sunday Jump, an open mic in Los Angeles's Historic Filipinotown. Her work has also been published in numerous publications including *KQED Arts*, *The Offing*, *Jacket2*, AngryAsianMan.com, and *Action, Yes!*, as well as anthologies such as *Empire of Funk: Hip Hop and Representation in Filipina/o America* (Cognella Academic Publishing, 2014) and *Namjai: An Intergenerational Tribute Anthology of Bay Area Asian Pacific Islander Poets* (The ReWrite, 2013). Her second book *Like a Solid to a Shadow* was published in 2017 (Timeless, Infinite Light). She earned her M.F.A. in Writing from CalArts, and has a B.A. in Ethnic Studies with Honors from UC San Diego. She is an Assistant Professor of English at Skyline College in San Bruno, CA and is the sixth Poet Laureate of Santa Clara County, CA. Janice loves playing with stuffed animals, runs races occasionally, and frequents local, small mom + pop coffee shops. You can learn more at janicewrites.com

Philippine American Writers and Artists, Inc.

PAWA

P.O. Box 31928
San Francisco, California
94131-0928

www.pawainc.com
pawa@pawainc.com

REFELECTIONS: READING FOR THE YOUNG AND OLD
edited by Penélope V. Flores (2002)

WHISPER OF THE BAMBOO:
An anthology of Philippine American Writers and Artists
edited by Penélope V. Flores, Allen Gaborro (2004)

FIELD OF MIRRORS:
An anthology of Philippine American Writers and Artists
edited by Edwin A. Lozada (2008)

THE PHILIPPINE JEEPNEY: A FILIPINO FAMILY METAPHOR
Understanding the Filipino American Family
by Penélope V. Flores with Araceli N. Resus (2008)

GOOD-BYE VIENTIANE: UNTOLD STORIES OF FILIPINOS IN LAOS
by Penélope V. Flores (2005, 2010)

REMEMBERING RIZAL: VOICES FROM THE DIASPORA
A collection of pieces by Rizal and writers inspired by Rizal
edited by Edwin A. Lozada (2011)

THE FIRE BENEATH: TALES OF GOLD
by Almira Astudillo Gilles (2012)

TO LOVE AS ASWANG: SONGS, FRAGMENTS, AND FOUND OBJECTS
by Barbara Jane Reyes (2015)

FLIPS 2015
A Filipino American Anthology, A Reprint
edited by Serafin Syquia, Bayani Mariano
Introduction by Juanita Tamayo Lott (2015)